We Sailed on the Lake

BUNNY

We

Sailed

on the

Lake

Bill Carty

BUNNY, an imprint of Fonograf Editions
Portland, OR

First Edition, First Printing
BUNNY02

Published by BUNNY c/o Fonograf Editions
www.bunnypresse.org
www.fonografeditions.com

Distributed by Small Press Distribution
SPDBooks.org

ISBN: 978-1-7378036-7-6
LCCN: 2022947437

... in the night, imagining some fear,
How easy is a bush supposed a bear!

A Midsummer Night's Dream, Act V, Scene 1

Poem

Bear took a walk in the woods and found a banana.
He liked the ring of it. (It was a telephone.) He thought

it nice to chase that sound. A parrot from a palm said
Over there in French and made bananas dear to him.

What? Through language he had never spoken?
There were many words for the words he was given.

There was *baba* and *nana*. There was living far
and living near. There was the trick of making this

from that. Which felt like a rush. Like he'd hardly been
a cub at all. Was never told *Don't put that in your mouth.*

Or, young again, had finally learned to part honeybee
from its sting. So his heart went *brrring, brrring*

through the forest. And we are left to hear it leave,
like a laugh does. Or be left, like a rind.

Greenspan

Wanted something, lost it,
then found it in the yield curve,
sensed the future's plotted swoon

or swag, one lone drunk sipping
from the mermaid fountain,
dark rush of clocks

come to coerce evening,
that misnomer—show me the day
that really ended at the level.

I view the graph from above.
It's a line now,
last red streak in the sky

before some recession settles
beneath the concrete benches
of the esplanade. It's cold.

A couple leans on the rail.
Are they taking a picture, or looking
at a picture they've just taken?

Orange vesters clog the path ahead.
To be safely seen or out to sell?
I want to know exactly what

I'm staring at. Neon blue sign
in the window of the vision clinic.
Song from shop speakers as I pass,

one of those gold standards in which
love must have been invented.
I'm down here below the city,

above water, climbing into the arcade
where I refuse to make a purchase.
I'm not carrying anything home tonight.

No one I know is sick enough
for balloons, or if they're sick,
they're not telling. Of course,

the answer's always flowers.
Who wouldn't mind some life
in this room the leaves blow into?

What do you call it? Some say *foyer*,
but it's nothing so romantic, just one door
with another door beyond it.

Garland

All books have gifts.
This book gives me "enfiladed rooms."
Yes, *how terrible to be locked in boxes,*

but when one room is strung upon the next
I want to walk further into the party
until it opens on the railyard.

There goes the last commuter.
It's been a long day considering
all we dressed up for.

And where's the slim credenza
of my mislaid cocktail?
Tomorrow too, still waiting

where we left it, like a list
to walk into? I lift an imagined drink
in empty hand as we move

backward through the festivities,
so concerned with elbows
I hardly notice faces.

Outer Lands

I'll tell you the story. I was walking
the outer edge of the outer lands

where sporadic signs staked in dunes
warned to keep distant from the mammals;

in fact, there were critical acts in place
to enforce non-molestation,

but between me and the sea
a seal appeared to be having a time of it,

rocked and moaned in a deepening berth
as if trying to summon momentum

to roll down the beach toward water.
In short, it seemed stuck and—it's never far off

in the imagination—dying. I thought
I should bring sea to the seal. I filled

a detergent bottle at the surf and called
the seal "buddy." "You okay, buddy?"

I said, as the tide went this way, then that,
with no sense of intention. An hour before,

I had encountered a friend on this beach,
both of us having walked through our pasts

to that moment. Now he was gone
and I was supposed to be in the mountains

but the mountains were on fire.
From the highway that morning

I watched smoke plumes rise
in each far valley and drove past my exit

straight for the coast, straight into
this story where I gathered

armloads of kelp, making a damp bed
for the seal. Increasingly, my efforts

bore the whiff of not science,
but ritual. I consulted the experts

I wasn't too embarrassed to ask.
On my phone I found a video

of a seal snared in Ocean Shores,
two cops hunched above it, jabbing

at tangled fishing lines with utility knives
as the animal lurched, as the cops jolted

from its teeth. A crowd in sweaters gathered
as the camera narrowed to tattooed flames

on a bicep clenched around the seal.
Beyond this, straggling clouds from Constable

on the horizon, bright light at their edges
reflected in mud. Then one officer

moved toward the SUV, retrieving a club, I feared,
though he returned with a stick and wire loop—

one for the dogs they don't shoot, presumably.
He fastened the catch at the seal's neck

and drove its head into sand until the body stilled,
suddenly submissive. What looked like choking

wasn't—this time—and the line was cut,
and the catch was loosed, and the seal's

arched back bounded for ocean. The algorithm
urged me further: a sea otter pup rescued

by blond hero in board shorts; a stranded whale
in Weymouth; a lone porpoise found

in a British farmer's field fifty miles from
the ocean. Here's the thing: I was looking

at the way things had happened in the world
for evidence of how the world would happen.

Which never works. Each day bears
its crucial variance. And I knew this,

practically had it written on a coffee mug,
but when I was there, and when there

was then, I had to say *stop*—and let red
fill the harbor, and let red wash the shore,

and vow never to touch another living thing
for fear of how my being human might kill it.

The Documentarians

We make wide arcs around the children
playing in the surf
tap the little yellow box
of focus

tiny sun
to get the light right
not so much light
that the surf looks washed

cloudy in the shot
we want the background rocks and strangers
correct
not too close, not too busy

you point and tell them where to look
I hold a thumb
to the screen the position tips
the scale of light

on these bodies
(we love them, the children
in the photo
their bodies being circled

to get the light right)
we love their acceptance
as we pass
closed playgrounds

juice box straws
buried in bark mulch
lights blinking
on empty sidewalks

we hardly find a door
uncobwebbed
chanting the fuzz
off my mouth one day

in a crowd I want you here
listening to the neighbors
get a little loose
listening to rain drown

the pollen
rain slick on the hides
of small creatures
creatures

we've freighted
with meaning all spring
we've freighted plot
on something as simple

as what happens
at the birdfeeder
and where
was the president

my child asks
when something bad
happens
hiding sorrow

in profit, I say
probably afraid
yes, very bad
I add

yet
completely worldly
and it was only
one day

hard to say so
when each lasts
this long
as long as rocks

The Rocks
they are called
in one painting
by Van Gogh

and they do seem
quite specific
when I turn
to see them in the sun

Domestics

In the Four Aces Diner the coasters were lacquered playing cards,
ill-designed but apt to theme, and our mugs tottered over each long edge
as I absent-mindedly nudged mine back and forth between my thumb
and index finger, trying to find the place where coffee didn't spill,

but there was no balance point; this was a puzzle to live with, not solve,
then it was time to go, utensils piled and napkins tented on syruped plates,
each abandoned coaster a different suit, one for each of us four,
and I was last to stand and leave my club behind. It was the weekend

before I moved south for grad school, and we drove again to the confluence,
walked cross-stream along the dam's iron rail, headed west
across state lines. These were the friends who knew me best,
could say "you have a way with people" and "you don't like people at all"

in the same breath and understand there to be no contradiction,
just moods and modes, ways of passing days, say, carrying around a copy
of *Middlemarch*, not reading *Middlemarch* at all yet wanting someone
to ask you about it. Our house we called the Bus Stop, at the fringe of town,

beside a sign for county transit, though we were the only house along
that stretch and strictly drove cars—I'm not sure I ever saw a bus even slow.
K had moved in with me, then Andrew with Claire, rent was halved but the energy,
as they say, maintained: we danced around each other's schedules, played

domestic roles, rotated dinners and cleaning chores—I baked my first focaccia,
learned what to do with leeks, how to grill an aubergine. As summer closed
we quit service jobs en masse to chase down swimming holes, long hikes full
of gentle needling about how I'd managed to apply the future so haphazard,

following deadlines but not desire, no sense of place besides its abstract cousin:
anywhere'll be fine, I think, thanks. I'd made one June loop around the country,
written faux Beat poems made true, I thought, by Native place names. Though
I claimed to love the road, I needed somewhere to be, to stay. I made a final trip

to the bookshop beneath the waterwheel, though I knew I'd know the used
stacks' titles, grabbed a six pack to split before a party at the fringe of campus,
where a soon-famous brother-sister band mangled and bashed new-old blues
in the basement. I remained in the gravel drive, "catching up," "saying bye,"

pouring a beer or five in plastic cups arranged like a triangular tree and placed atop
a piece of plywood spray-painted with a black-stenciled head of Che, red base coat
concealing the Greek letters of the house from which it was stolen, the hockey house,
and they could have killed us with their sticks, but didn't, and we escaped down

side streets, holding the board to my Volvo's roof. On this night, I chased
errant ping pong balls to the spotlight's edge, but soon rain meant the match
had ended, everyone spilled inside as the music finished,
and we headed home, lit a fire on the porch, and I watched flames reflected

in the kitchen window like I was looking for something I'd left inside,
half-turned from the others. In the morning, I said nothing much to K, nor Claire,
would rather leave quick than make a scene. What can I say? I lived like the future
would happen to me and carry others with it, but knew for once that lie,

and lying made me quiet. I waved, turning left out the driveway, then left again,
then south along the river, hours later catching beltways through the seaboard's
suburbs, Discman on my lap so it wouldn't skip, switching an old CD for new,
everyone clapping, half-shouting choruses. It seemed less detached, more communal,

with a whiff of tent revival that, like any god, made me nervous. One motel night,
another drive, and I arrived at my off-beach sublet, a single-story house
on a block of stilts, two stone tosses from the ocean. I hung the only art I'd packed:
a print of Monet's "Impression, Sunrise." Orange-gray scene like a headache

I remembered, hiking the arm of Mount Ascutney in the haze of Quebec fire,
K and I watching hang gliders launch from the peak—insanely, we thought—
toward what they knew was the river valley's bottom. So I was back at school,
a child shocked at every clock, dodging red lights through strip malls on my way

to campus. I presumed the sunrises to be amazing, though never saw a single one,
only setting light from the parking lot outside the laundromat where I read *The Years*,
awaiting cycles. I went to class, taught some too, but mostly walked where things
were sandy, drafting letters north more tone than feeling, impressions

gleaned from poem or film, parked outside a closed café, connected to wi-fi,
checked some scores, and never sent the letters. My inbox gave some sense
of what was churning: Andrew and Claire tripping Europe, K seeing another friend
with a suddenness that meant everyone, save myself, must have seen it coming.

Offshore, a hurricane was forming, green-screened forecasters charted course,
tracing variable arcing paths, a heat map of perspective power. The next day
I half-slept in a radar's pinwheel loops, then headed to the bar where the TVs
had been switched from sports to weather, got a sense from eyes raised

behind tilted pints that what would come was real, and headed home
with no plan of action. I didn't know the wind, and as the bartender said,
didn't have the accent. A neighbor caught me in the morning, said last time
the water was "freezer high," and nodded toward the intracoastal.

"That's where it comes," she said. "Bet you had your eye on the ocean."
In the morning I drove to school to observe another class, "teacher training,"
watching a professor skip the assigned translation for stories of his white youth
in Buffalo. The bartender from the pier was there, older than me, I knew,

in school getting her bachelor's. Nicole, I learned, and said I'd see her later at the bar,
which I did, sitting on the deck beside a row of empty bottles. Chatter swirled
toward crimes to come, whether plywood saved glass or signaled abandonment,
an invitation. Nicole came around and asked, "How you doing?" as no one had,

nor had reason to. I said I'd taken the rugs off the floor, piled chairs
on the dining table, said I might leave at dawn for northern cousins, though I
didn't trust my car farther than I could throw its engine. She was headed
in the morning for a friend's in town, offered a ride and a place to crash,

if the storm "went that way," as they said it would. So at eight, I hopped
in her car as the early surge began to crest, reaching the stop sign pole
at the nearest intersection. At her friend's, we waited for an hour on the porch
before he woke, then went inside and made coffee. "Useless," he said,

noting we lacked PFDs, LSD, no fun to get us through the weather.
Election signs buckled in the wind; a birthday garland blew off the neighbor's.
Nicole and I scrolled photos on our phones, chose a date and shared the nearest faces,
so I learned of Jonah's threats, Jackson's humor, Malcolm as who-could-have-been.

"Corinna, Corinna" came on a mix, K's favorite song, more branches snapped,
and we retreated. The TV on, we sat and smoked, watching a woman claw at the roof
of her coffin. When the TV cut, things got worse, we filled fresh water in the tub,
and though it was hardly noon, gathered batteries and candles. I tried to read a book

and doze, but then things weren't worse. Things had stopped. The eye, we said,
must be more to come, then walked outside and realized there wasn't. The storm was
gone, veered inland west, and what seemed a pause meant truly ending. Rain pooled
a bit in the street, and we decided—was it too soon?—to walk north and find out

what had happened. A downed powerline veered us toward a mini-mall,
and we passed a restaurant whose lights were on, two brothers inside had stayed
to protect their lot, now making meatballs and spaghetti. We bought a bottle,
poured sauce on bread, and ate on a curbstone. Policemen rolled in unmarked

patrols; people descended from their attics. On the walk home
Nicole's friend checked car doors for open locks, and I ducked in the bushes
to piss on a pile of cardboard. As we squeezed through a fence, I dropped the wine,
glass and red splattered at Nicole's feet. A quiet second and then the second

itself disappearing. Back at the house, I followed her toward the bath,
wet a rag, and when I turned, we kissed, though her palm never left my sternum.
"Let's not," she said, "ruin a good storm with bad decisions." I drifted to sleep
on the couch as the neighbor children shouted out back, playing with a box

of puppies. When I got home a lizard sunned itself at the foot of my steps,
the point from which the flood receded. The next day, planes refilled the sky,
wood-chippers whirred with fallen branches. In weeks ahead, I'd go back
to the bar, watch a game, stay later as my team kept winning. The bar

would empty, the game would drag, Nicole would say, "I'm done for the night,"
and head to the upstairs apartment but leave a pair of long-necked domestics,
the TV still on so I could watch from the deck, then hand me the remote
I'd drop in the mailbox. When the season ended, my team had won—a team

that absolutely killed, my mother said, her father with near-misses. Two weeks later
the bar closed; the hurricane had done some damage to its pilings. I moved
from beach to town, and with an eye back north made what I see now
were unconvincing phone calls. It was never my intention to feel there at home,

but that's where I was, and I made a script of my surroundings. The neighbor's house
was rented for a teen soap opera: one week I'd drive by and wave to John,
the next week the color would be different, planters lining the sidewalk, the door
newly coated, then painted back, a seasonal wreath marked passing time.

I sold my car to a fisherman who only needed to get as far as home, stayed silent
as the workshop teacher said to a classmate's essay, "No one's going to care—
or they may pretend, but they won't be buying." I saw Nicole once, the following
semester, in the library café at a lunchtime reading. As I read, I saw her pass

through the lobby, then pause to listen. I finished my poems, then moved
to the back of the room beside her, eyes down, scanning the periodical shelf
until the last applause, when she turned and said, "I liked it, but you know
it's not for me," like someone who understood attention to be a simple kindness.

How to Walk in the Snow

I've done a demonstration
where I head directly
across the lake

to the market
and meet Mike
who I haven't seen in ages

last fall he was living
on a commune
but just bought a house by the river

he's happy
now he's trying to
commercialize that as well

he has a company
what kind exactly
I don't know

sometimes
I really listen
and sometimes

all talk
is an insubstantial
flurry

I relace my boots
and head back out
it's almost like

to cross the lake
you've got to make each step
pertain to water

The Image

Picked up a glove
from a bush
and found
a hand inside.
I didn't feel

so lonely anymore.
I felt a little
spooked, honestly.
We were shaking,
we'd just met,

and I couldn't
extricate myself
from the pleasantry.
So I brought
the hand home

and put it on ice,
like something
I had to preserve,
though forgetting
was what I needed.

We Sailed on the Lake

We sailed on the lake before the storm

I felt my hair stand on end
and saw this in others

a family in tinfoil hats
weren't disturbed
by the forecast
of lightning

the water calm
golfers settled into hip sockets
doctor's orders to keep
synovial joints in motion

each time I asked
'is it safe?'

I ruined everyone's fun
for fear, my own
I didn't dare

carry mortality
into deep waters
where the gar swim

I wanted to go to shore
I wanted to eat again

we would go shopping
we would take the pig home
find a pencil-thin vein

of meat through the loin
the rest was fat
to sputter on the grill

we'd been taken by the butcher
who lived
we figured
where fat was good

the dog unhinged
the bone that let his jaw
drop to the floor
the only pose more sad
than death

could you imagine

my friend wished for, on occasion
his pets to disappear

he did so in the name of vacation

between himself and every
afternoon in Mexico
a dog guarded the jetway

he said to me
across the flames
'I'm firing blanks'

I hadn't asked how
he was doing

his silver sedan
was red with sunset
and I was fine imagining

we hadn't begun this
conversation

'feels like rain' I said
he said 'so no children
for now'

it was natural and otherworldly
on the hood of the car
the way only light

can bring an end to itself

I looked toward the shore

a rope swing tied
to the hollow branch
no one knew
was hollow

a distant road
glimpsed through the trees

the intermittences of travel
flash of an Aldis lamp

was there a game?
a speech on TV?

light rain hit the coals
and smoked

the storm had missed us

evening ceded all
its momentum

we found the butcher
in the forest picking leaves
from his sweater

the deck lit altar-like
with citronella

my friend tossed his thesis
on the flames
an anthropologist

in an awning of light
we played dice over
the body

the game was
roll and roll
until two eyes appear

someone would win
and take the head home
they would make cheese

come morning we'd pay
in thankless tasks
of tidying

in the dark
dock joints creaked to their gods

until one bolt
was cast from its bracket
into the reeds

likely lost forever

the whole enterprise
finding relief
in its absence

I wonder how the day would have gone
had we followed instructions

I'd almost forgotten
electricity

but it was there again
at the follicles

I stabbed the last pickled beet
on my plate

the last green sheep had gone to bed

the butcher buttoned
his black-checked shirt
and fastened his blood-red apron

his moustache was a century old
and more serious than I remembered

he walked off down the road
because every single day
work begins

even the sun
makes the same commute

you could believe me

or stay here all week
and follow it

the butcher a mile off now
crying
'she was my queen!'

forgive me

I'm only as human
as the last place
I've slept

forgive us

when we protect ourselves
in forms
that might appear
unloving

Pears Poem

A box of pears
arrives with instruction:
unwrap foil,
test for softening

at stem,
take a bite
and let what
can't be caught

drip onto
the silver
you've torn.
Leave it there

to follow the moon.
Step back
and ask
what the moon

is doing
in your kitchen.
The moon
that is not a poem

or rock
or face . . .
Do you mind it there?
Thank you.

The Marshes Have No Memory

Man drove horse hard. Gray thoroughbred,
half-brother to Guillotine. One day:

heart attack. Reins dropped. Carriage
wrecked. The horse collapsed. No marsh

remembers its avocets. Egg thieves lust
from the embankment built first to foil tides,

disassembled next to upset landing ships.
Of which the marshes have no memory,

knowing only how the huge sun participates
in fields of datura. How light steps unblemished

through vexations of prickly ash. Over the marshes.
And then the marshes themselves move on.

South Lake Union

In the megalomaniac's playpen
an artist fashions masks
atop the papier-mâchéd husk
of a shopping cart while
a programmer glides north
toward the lake blowing a kazoo
to summon ancient marshlands.
The earth turned over
in praise-worthy hill-raisings,
last century's technocrats
re-graded slopes of red
currant and partridgeberry,
while today's credulous
ventures aim billions
toward deep space or sea,
find delight in the underwater
click-through fantasia,
small portals in the window
of a coffee shop, bus ads urging

the to-be-hitched to form
a registry—enlist for a new
casserole or gaming console,
perhaps champagne flutes
to toast sacred songs
of the muses. Outside,
I pivot like desperate business,
pay two bucks for the non-profit
weekly, a few coins sweating
against my thigh, I find
a fountain for them,
toss as a tip or poker chip
with a wink for the fountain fish,
who come to it together,
a kiss. A pair at the bar
discuss the new boutique,
their work shirts are apt to task,
they boast a half dozen
perfunctory pockets.
The label reads not just China
but Guangzhou,
"radical transparency"
being the start-up's line:
You can go online and see
the smiling, sewing faces.
A student told me his family home
was there, since razed
for the airport's expansion.
His uncle sits at one end
of the runway with a dummy cannon,
scaring off the gander.

Some geese hold fast,
eager to glimpse our anxious,
pestilent species. Hey,
that's us, that's how it begins—

we arrive and reveal our age
too quickly. It's easy:
count backward from
now until the beginning
of Hesiod's *Works and Days*,
my copy's cover a scratched print
by Anne Carson titled,
"But Often Backward Turning,"
a bearded man in folded
robes—he's got the ancient
side-eye native to owls.
You'd be skeptical too
the first time you saw someone
turn chaos to atom. I'm watching
the sky sort itself out, herd
clouds toward the base
of the hill, herd seaplanes
into the bowl of the lake.
At the red light, a man waves
a wand in the intersection,
Angel Olsen singing in my ears,
I'm looking out the bus window,
hungry. Someone's carrying
the ubiquitous pink box
that must mean cupcakes.
Blessed sugars in their ages,

ours being that which builds
towers atop car repair shops.
And please say a prayer
for the Guitar Center.
No, I think that's still there—
the urge for song.

The bus radio beeps: a girl
is missing, pink boots
with green apples, another
with no shoes, one blonde,
one red, this is what
they were wearing,
this is the address
they are absent from.
And that's it—the chatter
stops. The bus chugs
up the hill and I'm late
for my connection.
The man in the seat
in front of me caught it.
I saw him running;
I saw him board;
he wanted it more.
Inhaling exhaust
from the Whole Foods vent,
I wait and watch
the passing traffic.
The flock abides,
not cheerful exactly,
but not so harried

as to make a fuss.
They fold the sun
into company umbrellas.
Which are yellow.
Which are free. Look how
they flaunt their trust
for one another.
I left my van unlocked
for just one night
and in the morning
my trust was gone . . .

Above, flat March light,
and beyond that I'd have
a hard time buying
some holy spirit within
the cloud-shroud doling
justice. But I'll believe
in any hero who needs
a grapplehook to pull herself
from bed in the morning.
This much I've gleaned
from a sidewalk preacher:
"Be careful what you indulge in.
I myself do the same thing."
I get it. I get a lot from this book
on Scandinavian deathkeeping.
"To hunt for misplaced things
is never an effective use of time,"
says a Swede named Margareta
who has obviously never scoured

the gentrifying city
for the Ethiopian restaurant
of her marriage dinner.
Many gyro shops have gone to sea
in the name of techne.
I guess what upset me most
was that I never saw a person.
I saw a concept form like weather
at the south end of the lake.
I saw lanyards on rain jackets
and lanyards on pea coats
and a pile of haphazard
traffic cones coated with glitter
like the most exciting thing
had just happened.

It was the fifth generation
Hesiod could do without—
Iron Age—days and nights
of trouble, small occasions
of property crime, the type
that send the fearful
to message boards.
As a downpour arrives to defeat
the last pedestrian,
red lights of an ambulance
flash in the coffee shop.
A Michigan Wolverines
sweatshirt left drenched
on a bench at the bus stop.
On the flat plate of a streetlamp

a crow makes a meal out of
whatever plus tortilla.
The last word was the hawk's
as relayed by the heron:
It was pathetic, as they fled,
how they left their hats
behind in the rain.

Patriot

Receipts balled
in my pocket
I like the odd way

they narrate
the impossible day
of which

you remind me
inside
we carry words

that keep
refusing to work
watchful

wearing stripes
of sun
now the blinds

are raised
and we
are the parade

I grip
a small flag
I've held

so long
I forget
I was given it

Whenever I Am in the Vicinity

"Many were the thoughts / Encouraged and dismissed..."

William Wordsworth, *The Prelude*

Blinds drawn I know

I'm far from home

        I'd never

blot the light like this

if I lived here nor paint

the walls this gray

where I've hung

the Singer Sargent print

        El Jaleo

too big for the museum's thieves

or not enough of a landscape

dim scene empty chair

a few guitars and music

in this room I read about

        the wind

about long nights of unsleeping

if you've studied the great non-sleepers

you'll have sighed into

Lorca's *ni mi casa es ya mi casa*

and you'll know the wind

moves everywhere

decides what to destroy

                or preserve

of our coastal dwellings

salt-lashed marsh shacks

and driftwood castles

it's said at the end

the whale is winner

                but really

              it's water

that takes the parking lot

takes the beach where the children

buried themselves

like clams for the bake

where saltwater seeps

through sand from

an imperceptible source

              tonight

I could have and then did

make dinner and watch a movie

about a father who wants

to sit down for a meal

with his wife and daughter

but finds himself

choking out the bad guys

with a broomstick

                             like weather

                             these fictions

find a way in

the blessing gentle breeze

the blue room's violence

always streaming

our good knights can't

resist breaking the idyll

even Wordsworth

noted he lived in a time

of the oppressed and among

                             the oppressing

yes see how the breeze can cradle

                    a tyranny

how wind coos against the surface

of artificial life and whatever

you'd call this poem

at the beginning in the end

it can't avoid imparting some half-

consciousness to what we know

                         is unfeeling

                         Nature

we've seen rage having escaped

the city and thought

it was a tad dramatic

to name our trip an escape

when it's a wanna-get-away

when it's only right with winter en route

to turn to wandering clouds

some floating things

though high deep thoughts

                         are there

liberty and abstruse

                    mornings

44   Bill Carty

you wake

determined to walk the whole jetty

and bring a scrap of Lispector

the terrible duty is to go to the end

which seems a bit vivid

so you check on the old bar

fashioned from street signs

in the beach town

where you lived and learned

how climate might make a place

history

at the harbor I watch boats

settle in their moorings

I hear a noise behind me

on the empty street

but it's only music

an accordionist on a bicycle

I take her tune with me

I used to borrow

freely

would simply float another's vessel

from the dock at night

in fourteen lines Wordsworth

makes the boat his own

slight sonnet of dispossession

                    poor Shepherd

                    I'm sorry

it's just the stars and their multiples

we can't spend all night

making crises from

whatever is knocking

in the home gas lines gables

or the quiet insulation

keeps the wind outside

while the hero in the kitchen

scrolls financial records

conclusions drawn but unexplained

                    this ovular

                    rod taps

                    the sill

some old custom to leave

the window cracked in storms

before the house explodes

though it's not pressure that does it

it's the lift of the roof the carapace

         aloft

         in the movie now

a drone strike leaves

its black mark on the desert

         once

I thought no war could start

if we stood out here at the edge of things

but then I drove home through

the states that elected the bomber

found a dreary winter basement

to watch two wars on television

green flashes from the embassy roof

the other panning black and white

walking among the graves

a historian speaking of trees

         as witness

         suppose

I send my daughter from here

toward the year 2100 but can't

by fiat grant her a moral life

it's her birthday and each red dot

is where a bomb fell

not enough viscera in the color

on a map in a bar graph in the street

a pneumatic tube counts

cars leaving the zoo concert

a plane makes its banking turn

high above IKEA should we skip

all that's obvious

for the action sequence

                              another evening

                              whiled away

                              writing

an email "I just resent it"

but I don't begrudge a thing

what I meant was "sent again"

"see you soon" to so many people

I've come to see only the back of

they drift in the middle of the lake

                    they drift

in unsent correspondence

we might meet again on the seacoast

taffy stores and t-shirt shops

it could be anywhere

but it's more specific than that

colder like a world

without Bach or Belize

or a friend you learned was really

just a circumstance

                              the light that

                              lights the switch

                              that lights the

                              lamp flickers

in its plastic shell a flame in ice

a way to make the darkness warm

while even now on planet Earth

someone fashions a bell against

despair someone paints a mural

or fires hot air into the lifting

balloon and the film was from

a damp unfeeling place

yet there was allegory to its ferity

two types

of weather

the kind you run from

and the kind where it's best

to stay put

on Main St. a man hears the call

to prayer and lays a purple t-shirt

in the parking lot while another

shouts something about Waco

sidestepping them into the gallery

I fall from the canvas into

the whiteness of the wall

walking home

I duck

beneath hanging caterpillars

I mark the occasional dark glance

among us not that anything bad

would happen until it does

I would never have

believed

in a bike-by stabbing

but it happened to me

a yellow bike a street hung

with Spanish moss

then the muscle visible

letting in

the wind

like something of our politics

has me back on Tolstoy's digression

on bees which was no digression

at all simply the city captive

to the death of its queen

while the baby sleeps

in the next room with Tylenol

with traffic revving

at the four-way stop

one slight wheezing

cough

as soldiers approach the hideaway

my father at the fringe

of the march smoking

or not smoking

        that mist

on the lake lifts

there's Wordsworth

in the boat he stole

the camera drifts

gray walls of the Pentagon

the lens shifts

among hippies and then

among cops but this

isn't one fiftieth

of the story we must

        digress

        again

        but smaller

a single bee in the frame

its fuzzy thorax

two glass wings flying

into this room

which is now fully mine

and soon will lack one wall

> I'm on the set

> I've made I

> repair and fix

> I repair and

> fix and then

I take the blue tarpaulin away

American Camp

San Juan Island

I have caught the cold of my country, cold looks in boxes, street corner
to office window, car window to bus stop, and if anger is so curative,
I wish you could look at it, cure in it, your eye—

6 a.m., hail on tin, a bleary hour, ringing bells where sails bob, then:
There goes one of those herons!—

I bring a floppy sketchbook to the sea, tented on the bench beside me,
the field where I last saw black foxes—

the bookstore owner closes shop an hour early. *I see your beloved at the
market, but I hardly see your face.* It's election day. She says, *See you on
the other side*—

college friends text jokes about what we used to watch on television.
The show isn't important. It's the dread behind it—

on Main Street a mammoth exhaust, deep hungry rumbling swallows
my Civic. My Civic. I've made that much public, cruised a little bit of
practicality around town—

nodding to the guy walking by. To him, I'm the guy—

a message from a friend: "Here are the first few paragraphs. Hope
you're staying sane. Please let me know what you think"—

I'd wanted to write like Laney wrote "Laney was here" in blue spray
paint on the barn's styrofoam insulation—

why do I keep this? "There's a chair-shaped stone in the woods
of Pomfret"—

the contour is essential. The deer path follows it—

I look at my hand. Red. Bleeding? No, that's tomato—

"everything up for grabs." Someone running has their fortune, while
the other relies on "donors like me"—

inside with my coat on. Not saving money. "Gaining perspective"—

toward the year 2100—

a goof to care so much, I think, walking through the dark outside
the labs, trippy screen flares caught through windows of the
empty offices—

I'm a little turned around—

all day, couldn't think. Tried timing a walk with the weather. Still
ended up soaked. Wrote nothing, but this—

> *It was like the first time I ever saw a painting. I entered the bar and
> saw a painting of the bar on the wall to the right, and in the painting,
> I saw the door I'd just walked through, I saw the street I'd left behind.
> I saw myself walking through the city in still traffic. I entered the
> door painted on the wall there, and inside, saw a horse pulled by
> brushstroke through the park. I must get back to it. The eyes were real,
> the years were real, the nose—*

Genesis

is playing at the pizza place
follow you, follow me
last low light

over the industrial zone
warehouse closed
no longer manufacturing

its underwater
security strategies
or echosonic search

for fish
in the faded logo
on corrugated steel

a scuba diver swims
beneath three nuclear silos
white dotted lines

indicating where
intruders would be foiled
civilization en masse

spared
to think: a whole industry
devoted to peddling

segmented vectors
and just last night in class
I drew a dotted line

between
beginning and *end*
said something like

that's where the poem exists
on a whiteboard
in purple dry erase marker

impermanence being
the art's chief function
because forever is scary

and every flotilla
is beautiful on the horizon
until you ask what they're up to

A Row of Trees

I bend the toothpick back and forth until it snaps.
Other clocks are more accurate.

Appetite, earworms, the little flesh
of light upon everything at dawn.

Erratic nightmares in the greenbelt:
twig-stabbed dolls

and shot-up Datsuns.
On this page someone circled

"empirical" "enlightenment"
    "comprehensive" "ineffable"

then underlined
    a hot bath for Hector, returning from battle.

In order to sleep I call out the questions.
I ask (and repeat)

Who gave me these questions?
My parents behind me, asking,

When will you be back?
Who's driving? etc.

Some unsolicited side-talk:
Life isn't always pigeons.

Siren through the playground
where I read two lines in translation:

    a ball of air
    leaves a box

We follow the shore home.
Old money.

A dozen apartment buildings
named "blank on the lake."

Sunset now.
Now there's no sun.

Orange light finds the water.
It's the city.

I'm waiting in traffic
for the ducklings to pass.

No one has all night,
but no one wants to be a monster.

I put down the book.
Whatever is gained

from going to the country
will be gained in green.

You can't do that tonight.
We have company.

Private bus service
at the public bus stop.

One charter failed for good this time.
For good. *Finally.*

We root for this failure.
For ruined plans for the evening.

For evening, period.
For whatever people mean when they say it.

On the ferry I write a note:
Remember chiasmus.

A sunfish floats on its side.
Is it dying?

Flirting with surface?
No, that's swimming for him.

The dead sculptor's iron sold for scrap.
Bare earth now where the dragon stood.

St. George blank-palmed, no sword,
snail beneath his heel . . .

Is he reaching in the cupboard
for peanut butter?

He looks like someone
who is reaching.

Tarkovsky's horse stumbles
downstairs, breaks its leg,

and is speared
off-screen. In the gallery,

an artist crafts a tree
from dead trees but can't

get the rough edge right.
It turns out,

she tells me,
There's a doctor for everything.

Other clocks
are more accurate.

Dry bark breaks
into hexagons.

When I was stabbed I carried
the knife inside me

the way some shot people
carry bullets.

The way the poem carries
this worm inside it

inside it.

I know the risk you take
folding laundry in a yellow dress.

You fold some sunshine
in those clothes.

For *what haunts is home.*
For being told nothing

is worse than being told
what haunts is home.

For to hear *what haunts*
re-promised to someone else

and think
home.

I am one of those people determined
to circle the lake before dawn.

I am one of those gap-toothed people
silent about missing spaces.

For we do not know
how it governs.

For every solution entails
new questions.

For example.

Tiny icon I've smudged
on the touch screen.

Another way to bring home flowers!
The opposite of love

could be anything,
but especially

infrastructure
or *portability*.

Watermark on the ceiling.
Only centuries move this slow.

Rain came in, left, and left
its scar.

Leaving leaves such things.
Leaves leave this way too.

Seems a drag
but it's the speed

things happen.
Don't you get it?

I want to be around you
around people.

A comma
dips

its paddle
beneath

the line
of the lake.

Reflected in sliding glass
I'm outdoors in my slippers

and see trees through
the window. Trees through

the window and a light
back where I left it.

Remains—
they could be anything

as long as they're not
what they used to be.

Who gave me these questions?
These almonds.

This salt dish.
This honey bear asleep

on its head.
This mess of flies.

This wall of green.
A row of perfectly

symmetrical trees.
How odd they seem.

The Parking Situation

the season's gone
but everyone's got

the green field
in their vision

for tomorrow
tomorrow

for Thursday
for the weekend

I looked all over
almost tipped

the table
the dogmatic grid

ran through my head
that was forever ago

we made turns
came upon

a chain
to have been any old

solitary bird
then

tilt your head
this way

I do not wish
to be lost

A Crown for Laocoön

> "The scream had to be softened to a sigh ..."
>
> Gotthold Ephraim Lessing, *Laocoön*

"No Gas, No Coal" read the banner
taped to the Laocoön's marble base,
where two climate protesters super-glued
their hands then turned to pose
for the photograph I saw in the Sunday paper,
reading calmness, I think, in their faces,
perhaps even focus in the eyes

of the pink-haired youth in floral dress,
her ally an older man—
white goatee, ponytail, polo shirt.
I saw their faces beneath Laocoön's,
which strained against the serpents' grasp,
his famous scream or shrug
or sigh, and I

remembered us being there,
tilting wearily from jet lag in a Vatican garden,
having wandering rooms
in a crush of people before we paused
in the Octagonal Court. It was the air we needed,
and we faced this father
who still maintained, the audio guide explained, sculpture's

"imperative to beauty." I heard the word
"Laocoön" and recognized
its echo from an old cassette,
a name I'd heard a thousand times unknowingly—
high school, driving roads woven among quarries
that filled first with water,
then garbage,

granite blocks dynamited and shipped south
for monuments, customs houses, libraries.
Laocoön . . . martyred . . . misconstrued . . .
began the verse, and I turned
to tell you this sculpture was from the song,
but we'd been separated
by a crowd flocking toward an art historian.

I saw you propped against a column—
a little distant, a little tired, pregnant,
we'd just learned, and sick in it.
I drifted away a bit, as I can get panicked
in congregation, prone to ditch
a train at random stops, or skip the flight
and rent a car, plus summer's always

a little spacey—this last one,
on vacation in California,
our son refused to leave the playground
as we waited at the gate, in boredom
turning toward the lake then back
to the slide to find him gone,
disappeared into a farmer's market,

anxious moments before we heard the music stop,
then saw him approach holding the hand
of the guitarist. *He said you had beard,* she said,
so I told him 'Great, we'll find him then'—
And so we found Laocoön, bearded, twisting
from the snakes while I sat on the rim of a fountain
beside floating lilies,

as one tour group gave way to next,
new interpreters shuffling past—
each falling in line behind the first analysis,
Laocoön's, who speared
the hollow horse, stood back, and said,
"Let's leave it." Then
a clattering of hooves, a creature sense,

as the Trojans turned from horse to tide to spy
two coiling snakes crest the waves,
wrapping first around Laocoön's sons,
each struggling to free the other,
their shared fate sealed
in their father's failure.
The people of Troy took Laocoön's punishment

as proof, his spear as spite to divine gift,
then conjured wheels and ropes
to pull the horse through city gates.
Now I'm at the beach in a hammock. We have two kids;
we're here with friends,
and the children have just been given a talk
about sneaker waves. This threat

finds no purchase in their play, which lasts
through morning's marine layer
until afternoon's canned cocktails. Some parents stand
beside the kids at water's edge,
knowing water's edge is never edge for long.
Others sit in lawn chairs above the high tide line.
Last winter one friend's friend made the same escape,

and as her kids touched their toes to the tide,
the sea surged, her husband went after,
and his was the only body they found.
"His pity seems to float on them in a dim vapor,"
said Winckelmann of Laocoön's
mouthful of sorrow. A mist settles along the shore,
dampening the socks we've hung to dry

as our friend tells this story, and we say very little,
scrubbing pots with sand and seawater.
Laocoön brought his kids to the beach
for the ceremony. There was to be sacrifice,
a bull offered to the ax before the ocean
intervened. I remain safely ashore, swinging, anchored
at two points to a wind-twisted tree, one strap

lashed to its arched trunk,
another at a thick root, erosion-exposed.
Soon heat reaches shade, and I walk to the waves
among roiling pebbles, carry
some surf in my ears back up the beach, garbled thrash
of words underwater—"Bath time,"
I used to sing to our daughter,

"Bath time, hope it's not like last time,
when your mother put you in a bucket,
and you floated to the sea."
We tried to give advice.
Swim parallel to the pull.
Not against: out. And as time passed,
backwards, I pushed through it,

went with the current, found myself alone
again in front of the sculpture—
impossible to see behind, to get beyond
the rope. But I tried, tip-toe
on a single foot. And they were trying, the sons,
each lifting leg from plinth,
as if pushing from the ocean floor,

though there's no bottom to the myth, no clear reading
at its margins, the marble lit with flash, much around us
seeming cinematic: garbage collection, gulls, the crescent
of dawn we caught in the oculus. Why return
to this story with its tragic ending? Because
the grip of it. Because the hold we relinquish to narrative.
Because sculpture exists as commemoration, as decoration, as demonstration of skill,

or means to celebrate the wealth-slash-power of those who paid
the commission. Yes, art has its way of aestheticizing
the "thank you."
Or, in this case, the "no thanks." Because Troy
didn't trust Laocoön's vision. Didn't want to hear
"Beware Greeks bearing gifts." They'd already let the horse
deep in their hearts. At the harbor

in my hometown, there's a stone carved
too life-like: the faces a poor digitization, the mason
having traded affect for accuracy,
a father and two sons lost at sea in a fishing accident,
always a wreath there, a long summer day at beginning
or end, a wreck in the paper,
a pet missing near the quarry, an old friend's arrest

or overdose or both: once I saw two classmates
wrestling each other in the dirt beside the firepit,
then years later in the courtroom,
pinning who got the drugs from whom. Who got sick, got pain,
got the worst of it. And still—something artful
in their struggle, gauze of VHS tape
over everything, the way life leads first

through the fight of it (youth),
then the ash upon the clothes of it (time),
and if you make it up, make it older, the costumes change,
the ocean calms, and one substance given
to the pressures of light and depth becomes measurably distinct
from itself. Becomes two things.
Then a third. We watched

the water come in, mistaking the tops of rocks
for heads of seals.
We wanted desperately to spy a pelican or whale.
No boats came by. No sails
held all our wishes on board. But what if
there's something anatomically impossible
in the furrowed forehead,

in the arch of eyebrows—
so Darwin argued, though he allowed
some slip in truth for sake
of beauty. Much prodding,
much exegesis, reading Lessing on Laocoön,
reading Arnold on Lessing, yet nothing heard
from his loved ones—may they not speak

of his breath
and the bright words that crossed it?
Yes, a translation from shouting to silence.
A friend asks at the bar, "What are you thinking,
bringing a kid in here?"
But "here" is not the bar.
The baby's not been born yet. "Here"

is the world. The tragedies are at hand
(especially if you have reception).
Our daughter, seven now, brings a wine bottle
to the hammock, filled to the brim with sand.
Drink and be whole again beyond confusion.
We've taught her some toasts, taken her to watery places,
yet never one so warm as the womb

as we toured the ancient city, regarding death
at hand in a hundred frescoes.
Often we knew little of the story
beyond the scenes
as we saw them, we didn't know the endings.
I think nearly an hour passed before we reunited
in the square outside the basilica. Had we

seen it all? Had we meant to leave?
It didn't matter. The tickets—
mine showed a close-up of Aristotle's hand
in *The School of Athens*, held horizontal, emphasizing the particular—
would not permit re-entry.
A week later, we'd fly home. We'd pull into the driveway,
back up the car a little, re-maneuver.

But first, we moved past men hawking
selfie sticks and umbrellas.
I bought coffee from a stand, and we stood
for a moment beneath the shade
of an archway, then walked east toward the river
into a whole other country,
passing through days of which light is the measure.

The End

how can we go to bed
when we have so many dogs to look for

plus another chapter
you said one more

you said we had time
you said once upon a time

there was a monkey
and once upon a time

there was a bear
and an owl and the owl

had claws but not like
the photo on nana's wall

I don't like the song in her clock
or the birds all settling

at the shore in the dark
I don't want to float

out here anymore
paddle us back slow like a snail

a snail is most careful
a snail never drops his shell

Notes and Acknowledgments

Thank you to my family, Kat, Lise, and Emil, to my parents, Jeff and Sandra, to Peter and Jessica, for being alongside me during the writing of these poems.

Thank you Paul Hlava Ceballos, Kary Wayson, Gabrielle Bates, Ellen Welcker, Katharine Ogle, Jane Wong, Michelle Peñaloza, Constance Hansen, Alex Gallo-Brown, Keetje Kuipers, and Dujie Tahat, each of whom provided important feedback and conversation around these poems.

Thank you to Jeff and Adie and everyone at Bunny/Fonograf for your care and attention to the book.

Thank you to Laura Grey and Bella Bennett for the cover and book design.

Thank you to the Whiteley Center at Friday Harbor Labs and the Fine Arts Work Center in Provincetown, where many of these poems began. Thank you to Emily Hunt's "Active Listening" workshop, which provided a seed for many poems too.

"Poem" and "The End" both begin with lines from my daughter. Thank you, Lise!

The "enfiladed rooms" in "Garland" are the "enfiladed drawing-rooms" in Edith Wharton's *The Age of Innocence*.

The italicized section of "American Camp" echoes Georgia O'Keeffe's letter to Russell Vernon Hunter. Thank you, Clair Dunlap, for bringing this letter to our class.

In "Whenever I am in the Vicinity," "ni mi casa es ya mi casa" is from Lorca's "Romance Sonámbulo."

The title of "A Row of Trees" comes from Emily Hunt's poem "English." The lines "a ball of air / leaves a box" are from Nagata Kōi (translator unknown). "For we do not know how it governs" is borrowed from a letter by Philip Guston to Ross Feld.

"A Crown for Laocoön" owes a debt to Richard Brilliant's book *My Laocoön*.

Additional thanks to the editors at the following journals where some of these poems have previously appeared:

32 Poems: "Poem"
A Dozen Nothing: "Whenever I am in the Vicinity," "The Documentarians"
Best American Poetry 2022: "Outer Lands"
Denver Quarterly: "Greenspan"
Iterant: "Patriot," "The Parking Situation"
jubilat: "Genesis"
Kenyon Review: "Outer Lands," "We Sailed on the Lake," "The Marshes Have No Memory"
Moss: "South Lake Union"
Octopus Magazine: "Pears Poem"
Paperbag: "A Row of Trees"
The Seventh Wave: "How to Walk in the Snow"

About the Author

Bill Carty is the author of *Huge Cloudy* (Octopus Books, 2019), which was long-listed for The Believer Book Award. He has received poetry fellowships from the Fine Arts Work Center in Provincetown, Artist Trust, and Hugo House. Originally from Maine, Bill lives in Seattle, where he is Senior Editor at *Poetry Northwest* and teaches at Hugo House, the UW Robinson Center for Young Scholars, and Edmonds College.

FONO
GRAꟻ

Fonograf Editions is a registered 501(c)(3) nonprofit organization.
Find more information about the press at: fonografeditions.com.

BUNNY

1. Warren Longmire—*BIRD/DIZ [an erased history of bebop]* (print)
2. Bill Carty—*We Sailed on the Lake* (print)

Inspired by the work of the multitudinous artist Ray Johnson, BUNNY is an imprint of Fonograf Editions. Publishing a wide variety of works, BUNNY is looking towards the future while thinking about the past.